RULERS, SCHOLARS, AND ARTISTS OF THE RENAISSANCE™

LORENZO DE' MEDICI

Florence's Great Leader and Patron of the Arts

RULERS, SCHOLARS, AND ARTISTS OF THE RENAISSANCE™

LORENZO DE' MEDICI

Florence's Great Leader and Patron of the Arts

Lee Hancock

rosen central™

The Rosen Publishing Group, Inc., New York

Published in 2005 by The Rosen Publishing Group, Inc.
29 East 21st Street, New York, NY 10010

First Edition

Library of Congress Cataloging-in-Publication Data

Hancock, Lee.
Lorenzo de' Medici: Florence's great leader and patron of the arts/by Lee Hancock.—1st ed.
    p. cm.—(Rulers, scholars, and artists of the Renaissance)
Includes bibliographical references and index.
ISBN 1-4042-0315-X (library binding)
1. Medici, Lorenzo de', 1449–1492—Juvenile literature.
2. Statesmen—Italy—Florence—Biography—Juvenile literature.
3. Intellectuals—Italy—Florence—Biography—Juvenile literature.
4. Renaissance—Italy—Florence—Juvenile literature. 5. Florence (Italy)—History—1421–1737—Juvenile literature.
I. Title. II. Series.
DG737.9.H36 2005
945'.5105'092—dc22

                                                      2004010576

Manufactured in the United States of America

On the cover: Background: *Adoration of the Magi* by Sandro Botticelli (1445–1510). Inset: Lorenzo de' Medici

CONTENTS

INTRODUCTION: THE GREAT RULER AND PATRON

During the latter part of the fifteenth century, a ruler came to power in the state of Florence, Italy, who set a precedent that other world rulers strove to follow. Lorenzo de' Medici, a member of the famous political and banking Medici family, became famous as a ruler as well as for his passion for art, poetry, philosophy, sculpture, and books.

We know a great deal about Lorenzo and his actions in Florence through a variety of sources. Perhaps most important of all are the accounts of his life made by Lorenzo himself. Not only did he keep a personal diary in which we can read his most private thoughts, but he was also a great letter writer. He wrote letters to a great number of people, such as other important rulers, as well as to family and friends.

LAVRENTIVS MEDICES PETRI FILIVS

From the great ruling family of Florence, Lorenzo was the only Medici to earn the title "the Magnificent," a title that was used at the time of the Renaissance to show adoration to its subject for his or her accomplishments. Niccolò Machiavelli, in his *History of Florence*, would call Lorenzo, "the greatest patron of literature and art that any prince has ever been."

Luckily for historians, many of these letters still survive, as they are important to our understanding of what sort of man Lorenzo really was.

Historians who actually lived in Italy during the fifteenth century are another great source of information about Lorenzo and Italy in general. The books and opinions of such men as Francesco Guicciardini (1483–1540) and Niccolò Machiavelli (1469–1527) are very important in trying to find out the truth about Lorenzo and how his actions affected the lives of those around him.

Many other rulers have been very interested in the arts, too, but we know of them only for the way in which they ruled their respective countries. While their artistic interests are often mentioned, these are not a major reason why these leaders are remembered in history. With Lorenzo de' Medici, however, he is just as famous, perhaps more so, for his patronage of the arts as for his politics and his leadership. To find out why this is the case, we must look at the world into which Lorenzo was born and the emerging forces that had such a deep influence on him.

FLORENCE AND THE RENAISSANCE

At the beginning of the fifteenth century, during a period known as the Middle Ages, Europe was still very much ruled by the Roman Catholic Church. The pope, the head of the church, decided what was acceptable for people to believe; every part of life was ruled by the Christian religion. To question the church or its teachings was thought to be going against the word of God. But at this time, the church itself was very corrupt. Church leaders were often more interested in becoming rich than they were in following the teachings of Jesus. In this atmosphere of stagnation, some people began to look beyond the narrow boundaries of knowledge approved by the church. They looked to an earlier period, in

The study of the Greek sculpture the *Laocoön Group*, from the second century BC, would greatly influence Renaissance artists such as Michelangelo (1475–1564) when it was brought to Italy in 1510. In Greek mythology, Poseidon sent the serpents to strangle Laocoön, who was the priest of the sun god Apollo, and Laocoön's sons after Laocoön advised the Trojans to keep the gates of Troy locked against the Greeks' gift of the wooden horse.

which thinking and learning were praised rather than outlawed.

Perhaps the most important of these people was Italian poet and scholar Francesco Petrarca (1304–1374), also known as Petrarch. Being an Italian, Petrarch began to study the literature and art of ancient Rome. Although the church is known as the Roman Catholic Church, as the church was originally based in Rome, the ideas of the ancient Romans were very different from those that the fifteenth-century church leaders believed. Petrarch and other Italians began to explore the "classical" teachings and artistic works of the Roman civilization, as well as the thoughts of the ancient Greek philosophers. The Greco-Roman (meaning coming from Greece and Rome) cultures valued the place of man in the world and were more interested in man's life on earth. This was in direct opposition of the church's belief that the afterlife, based on the ideas of heaven and hell, was more important than thinking about how man could best use his time while he was still living.

This rediscovery of the ancient teachings and works of the Romans and Greeks became known as the Renaissance, a French word that means "rebirth." Scholars began to look to the past to build the future. By looking at the ideas brought forth in the ancient world, scholars hoped that this "rebirth" would bring in a new and exciting age for humankind.

THE HUMANISTS

One of the most important ideas to come out of the Renaissance was humanism, the philosophy that man is an important part of the universe. This may seem obvious to us now, but at the time of the Renaissance, it was a revolutionary idea. The church taught that God was all-powerful and man existed to worship God, live his life on earth without trying to better himself, and live a good life so that he could get into heaven when he died. Humanists, however, thought that man should try to improve himself during his lifetime. According to the humanists, man was created by God and should try to show that he was worthy of being put on earth. The ideal man was someone who always tried to learn more, be the best that he could at all things, and to always think for himself by questioning everything around him.

This way of thinking had a massive influence on the scholars of the Renaissance. But humanist ideas were not altogether new. The ancient civilization of Greece had produced many great philosophers— people who wanted to discover the truth about man's place in the world. One of the greatest of these philosophers was Plato (circa 427–347 BC). When Renaissance scholars began to rediscover the ancient writings of the old civilizations, the works of Plato became very popular.

Plato believed in what he called the Theory of Forms. He thought that every single object on earth was actually only a copy of the real, perfect item, which existed in some other dimension. So, for example, every chair that we ever see is not a "chair," but simply an imperfect reproduction of the original, perfect chair that we will never be able to see or touch because it is beyond our senses of sight and touch. For many who read Plato's work, this other world, where such things like the perfect chair existed, sounded a lot like heaven.

Plato died around 350 years before the birth of Jesus. As his writings could obviously not take into account the Christian philosophy that was so important during the time of the Renaissance, the humanists tried to join Plato's ideas with the teachings of Christianity. This philosophy was called neoplatonism. ("Neo" comes from the Greek word *neos*, which means "new").

NEW PERSPECTIVES IN ART

These neoplatonist philosophers believed that man was basically good and that if he acted like God, he could become godlike himself. Man should use all his worldly powers, glorify man and his achievements, and not be embarrassed by his mind or his body. Many artists of the Renaissance period portrayed this theme of glorifying man. Before the fifteenth century, many painters produced flat,

The Vision of the Chariot of Fire by Giotto di Bondone (1296–1297). Giotto was from Florence, and as a painter in the medieval period of art, his work is often considered to be a precursor to the Renaissance style. Giotto depicted many scenes from the life of Saint Francis. Here, the beloved saint appears in a fiery chariot at midnight to his brothers.

two-dimensional paintings. This style of painting, although popular at the time, did not show perspective—an object in the distance was the same size as an object in the foreground. When using perspective, the artist draws the image the way it is seen with the human eye—things in the distance appear smaller than things that are up close. For example, in pictures that featured castles, the people and animals in the paintings were shown as being the same size as the enormous castles.

A more realistic method of depicting images had been used in the classical worlds of the Greeks and Romans and so inspired the Renaissance artists to experiment with these rediscovered styles. It was not only painters who tried to make their art as true to life as possible. The Italian artist Donatello (1386–1466) produced a bronze sculpture called *David*. What was especially interesting about this piece was that it was the first large sculpture since the days of the classical civilizations of ancient Greece and Rome to show a naked human body. Interestingly, the person who commissioned Donatello to produce *David* was Cosimo de' Medici (1389–1464), Lorenzo's grandfather. As we shall see in the next chapter, Lorenzo wasn't the first Medici to support the arts. Cosimo's actions would have a deep effect on Lorenzo.

Before the Renaissance, portraying the naked human body in such a realistic way, as was done with Donatello's *David*, would have been un-thinkable. During the Middle Ages, many believed that art existed only to glorify God, the church, and Jesus. Works such as Dona-tello's *David*, which showed the beauty of man, were looked upon as being disrespectful to God. During the Renaissance, however, art was being enjoyed for its own sake, and many of the rich people in Italy wanted to own these new and exciting pieces of art.

Donatello's *David*, circa 1440, was the first free-standing, nude bronze sculpture since the Roman era. The biblical hero is standing over the head of the giant Goliath, whom he has just slaughtered. David's hat is thought to be straw, like one that a peasant would wear, and was meant to protect him from the desert sun. The laurel on the hat is thought to symbolize victory.

Patronage of the arts—giving financial support to painters and artists—became fashion-able among the wealthy. The money these patrons invested in the new styles of art meant that many beautiful works were produced in Italy during this time. As we will see, Lorenzo was perhaps the

Florence was established during Roman times where the River Arno converges with the Mugnone. This nineteenth-century painting depicts the bridges and banks of the River Arno from the famous Ponte Vecchio built in 1345. Florence during Lorenzo's time comprised town squares, twisting streets, and crowded tenements. Its population was around 50,000. Today, it still bustles as a center of commerce and culture, and its population is about 400,000.

greatest of these patrons. Many brilliant and famous artists such as Michelangelo and Sandro Botticelli (1445–1510) began their careers with Lorenzo's money and support.

FLORENCE ON THE RISE

The Renaissance began in Italy, with the city of Florence quickly becoming the center of this

new cultural explosion. To understand why Florence in particular should be the main focus of the Renaissance, we must look at the city's history and its state of affairs at the start of the 1400s. At this time, Italy was not the unified country that it is today. At the beginning of the fifteenth century, it was made up of independent city-states dominated by five major powers: Milan, Naples, Venice, the Papal States, and Florence. Despite being so close to each other, the five states differed greatly in the way they were run. Milan was dominated by a ruthless prince, Naples was ruled by a king, Venice was an unofficial dictatorship, and the Papal States were run by the pope. The pope also ran his array of domains with ruthlessness and total power from the capital city of Rome. However, Florence had discarded automatic rule by nobility, and had established a democratic republic in the style of the ancient Greeks. Many historians believe that the reason Florence was able to achieve this type of government was because the city had become an important business center.

Until about AD 1000, Italy was still ruled by what were known as feudal lords and nobles. These men ruled everyone and everything around them, treating the people who lived under them like slaves. But the lords eventually lost their power. The lords were not overthrown by other nobles during violent wars. Instead, they were removed from their positions of power by a clever type of businessman that was beginning to emerge in Italy.

Around this time, commerce and trade began to flourish, making some people very rich. Traders began to sell and trade their goods with Asia—the Orient and the Middle East—and later on with other parts of Europe. All kinds of goods were available and were traded, such as the luxuries of spices and silks from the East. The merchants, bankers, cloth makers, and craftsmen became very wealthy. As a result, some of them became very ruthless and ambitious. They envied the nobles' power and sought to get rid of them so that they, the merchants, bankers, and artisans, could have this power for themselves. They did not commit murder or violence; they were businessmen, not soldiers. But they did use their own particular skills, that of

Niccolò di Pietro Gerini, a fifteenth-century Florentine painter, depicts bankers in a fresco from the story of Saint Matthew. Florence was an important banking center, and Florentine bankers were known throughout Europe. The florin, Florence's gold coin, was considered of such purity that it was the standard currency throughout Europe well into the twentieth century.

business and banking, to remove the feudal lords from their seats of power.

The nobles were often in debt, so they looked to these newly wealthy men for loans of money. When the bankers lent money to the lords, the lords were made to sign a contract stating that if they could not pay back the loan, the bankers could take parts of their lands. The nobles' debts were often very big, and they had no chance of repaying the bankers. Instead of taking bits of the nobles' lands, however, the moneylenders lent the nobles more money, deliberately putting the lords further into debt. Over the course of about 300 years, the bankers had all but wiped out the nobles' fortunes and taken all their lands for themselves, making these bankers incredibly powerful and rich. The most clever and tough of these moneylenders were found in Florence. But the wealth and good fortune of the city was about to end.

THE RENAISSANCE CITY

In 1348, the bubonic plague swept into Florence. Known as the Black Death, this plague became the biggest disaster Europe had faced so far. Most historians believe that the plague originated in China and was brought to the West by infected rats on ships. One of the ways a person knew he or she had the plague was when lumps, or buboes, varying in size from that of an egg to that of an apple, began appearing on his or her body, often on the neck or in the armpits. Once these lumps appeared, the victim had only about one week to live. It's believed that the Black Death killed between 25 and 50 percent of the population of Europe. In Florence, it killed half the city's inhabitants.

Terrible though it was, the plague shaped Florence's future. Because the city was in crisis, the few remaining businessmen took control over the city, brought back some sort of order, and made themselves very powerful at the same time. These traders formed themselves into guilds—groups of men from the same industry who regulated their particular business. Because these guilds were so well run, commerce and trade became very successful and Florence became a great city once again. The Medici family was among the most successful.

A lead cross that marked the grave of a plague victim in 1348. The plague may have reached Italy when merchants returned to Genoa after being attacked at their trading station, Kaffa, located on the Black Sea. Plague-infested corpses had been catapulted over the fortresses of Kaffa. The merchants threw the bodies into the sea, but were infected in the process.

Guilds held great power. For example, in the year 1425, Florence's population was 60,000, and only the 5,000 members of the twelve guilds were allowed to vote. This was in keeping with the ancient Greek form of a democratic republic government that Florence had established. Democracy was strictly limited this way—it was not a modern-day democracy, like the United States—however, it did extend power to the middle class, which made Florence ahead of its time in this regard.

To make sure that no one person became too powerful, regular elections were held so that he could be voted out of office.

As Florence's democratic republic placed an emphasis on the public good, much importance was placed upon education, especially on learning the new—or rather rediscovered—thoughts and ideas of the classical Greeks and Romans. Students learned new and exciting ideas from the ancient worlds. One book, Ptolemy's *Geography*, became particularly important, as it explained the art of mapmaking. In *Geography*, Ptolemy (circa AD 90–170) invented the system of longitude and latitude, the grid system that we still use today to locate places on maps. The book also explained the concept of perspective, which was used by Renaissance painters.

The Florentines began to have confidence in the future of Florence, with its growing culture of learning and its democratic style of government. In 1390, the Duke of Milan announced that he intended to rule all of Italy by himself. All of the other republics in Italy fell to the duke, except Florence. By 1402, the citizens of Florence were exhausted from fighting the duke; the city was on the brink of collapse. But with the duke's sudden death, the Florentines came to realize that they were the champions of freedom, liberty, and learning.

Florence itself was the perfect city for this exciting age. It had large and open squares where people met to talk, gossip, and exchange ideas about the latest developments happening around them. The city's rulers also enjoyed the new, fresh ideas that were making the city a great place in which to live. But in this atmosphere of excitement, the city's rulers, the new class of businessmen, looked to use the Renaissance to enhance their images in the eyes of their fellow citizens, and indeed, to increase their wealth and power.

THE MEDICI FAMILY

1
3
4
5

Many subjects view their kings as great and powerful figures, even if they are unpopular as rulers. Yet the new ruling class of Florence, the businessmen, did not have this automatic respect from the people. The new elite were, in effect, normal citizens like everyone else. Businessmen began to hire painters, sculptors, and architects to design grand and beautiful monuments and artwork, in the hopes that the people of Florence would see that they were important and powerful men, worthy of the people's respect. Each man wanted to outdo his rivals; this attitude carried over into the business world. Rival families in Florence used ruthless and cunning tactics to gain more power and wealth than their competitors. To rise to the top, businessmen

The Medici family can be traced back to the twelfth century, yet Giovanni di Bicci de' Medici *(top)* (1360–1429), is considered the family's founder. A skillful banker and intelligent businessman, he was also known for being quiet and reserved. His son Cosimo "the Elder" *(bottom)*, also had his father's modest traits, but was the first to conquer Florence's political power and pass it on to his son. Piero *(right)* suffered from ill health for most of his life and came to power at age forty-eight. He was known for being considerate and scrupulous.

had to be very clever and ambitious. By 1402, there were two main rival families in Florence: the Albizzis and the Medicis.

The first member of the Medicis to set the family on its path to fame and glory was Lorenzo's great-grandfather, Giovanni di Bicci de' Medici (1360–1429). Giovanni was a great banker who steadily built up the family's fortune. But unlike the Medicis who followed him, he did not use his money to enter politics. Giovanni served for one term as Gonfalonier of Justice, the highest position in the government of Florence, but he devoted most of his time to the business of banking. As the pope's banker, he made a lot of money. Giovanni and his family also became very important figures. When Giovanni died in 1429, he left the business to his son, Cosimo de' Medici (1389–1464). In Italian society, the family was extremely important. Everything an individual member did was always for the greater good of the family as a whole. Cosimo continued to build up the Medici fortune and influence.

The Medici family was not the only important banking family in Florence. As was mentioned earlier, there was the rival Albizzi family. Fortunately for Cosimo, an opportunity arose that would bring about the ruin of the Albizzi family. The Albizzis had declared war on the Italian state of Lucca in 1429. Milan, one of the five major states in Italy, joined the war on the side of Lucca. The cost of paying for this large-scale war almost bankrupted Florence. After four years of war, Rinaldo, the head of the Albizzi family, signed a peace treaty that made Florence appear to be defeated. The Florentines felt angry and humiliated. In this atmosphere, Cosimo made his move against his rivals.

Cosimo let it be known that he was not happy with the way Rinaldo had managed the war. As Cosimo was an important man, people listened to him, and indeed many agreed with him. Having started his plan to stir the people against Rinaldo in 1433, Cosimo moved to one of his country villas to see how the events he had set in motion would turn out. Rinaldo was very angry with Cosimo for his remarks. Cosimo was summoned to the Palazzo della Signoria, the seat of the Florentine government. There, Cosimo was sent into exile to Venice. This was only a minor setback for Cosimo. He was still popular in Florence and this popularity would give rise to a pro-Medici government elected in 1434. As a result, Cosimo was brought back from Venice, the Albizzis were exiled, and Cosimo was appointed the new political leader of Florence.

Although he had government rules to follow, Cosimo did not mind bending these rules if it meant that he, and future generations of Medicis, could go on ruling Florence. One of the clever ways he bent the rules was by changing the electoral system. At first, all guild members who wanted to hold positions of power put their names into leather purses. Anyone whose name was drawn was appointed to the jobs. Cosimo set up a committee of ten electors (all of whom were his friends and allies) who picked the names out of the purses by hand. Cosimo made sure that only his friends' names went into the purses in the first place. With the friendly electors picking Cosimo's friends' names out of the purses, he could not lose. This system meant that the Medicis would remain in power.

COSIMO AND THE ARTS

Although Cosimo was a devious ruler and businessman, he had a genuine love of the arts and learning, which he described as "cultivating his soul." Since Cosimo was at least four times as rich as any other man in Florence, he could easily afford to spend money on the arts. He became a key figure in the revival of the studies of the ancient worlds and the first great Florentine patron of the Renaissance. Cosimo commissioned architect Filippo Brunelleschi (circa 1377–1446) to redesign the San Lorenzo Church in the city. The church was just one building in the area of Florence where Cosimo hired architects to design and construct new buildings. Michelozzo (1396–1472) built the Palazzo Medici for Cosimo and his family. Another church, San Marco, was part of the so-called Medici area.

Cosimo also had a passion for books. He employed hundreds of agents and scribes to find and copy ancient manuscripts, including works by such people as Ovid (43 BC–circa AD 17), Plutarch (circa 46–120 AD), and Livy (59 BC–AD 17). Cosimo may have spent more money on these manuscripts than he did on the Palazzo Medici. In 1444, Cosimo deposited 800 books at the San Marco Church, thus establishing the Biblioteca Marciana, the first public library in Europe.

Cosimo suffered badly from gout, an extremely painful illness that affects the joints and eventually cripples the sufferer. Gout has often been described as the "disease of kings" because it was associated with rich men who overindulged in rich food and drink. As we shall see, Cosimo was not the only Medici to suffer from gout.

The interior of the San Lorenzo Church in Florence. Built in the fourth century AD, it is the oldest church in Florence. San Lorenzo was the parish church of the Medici family. The exterior of the church is a stark contrast to its ornate and detailed interior décor, which earns it the title of Renaissance Church.

In 1464, Cosimo died of gout. Although he often didn't live up to the democratic ideals of Florence's republic, he was, in all but name, king of Florence. However, Cosimo was a popular leader. When he died, the citizens of Florence had the words *Pater Patriae* (Father of the Fatherland) inscribed on his tomb to show that they considered him the father of their land. As was the tradition, Cosimo's son, Piero, became the ruler of Florence.

THE BRIEF RULE OF PIERO

Piero (1416–1469) was forty-eight years old when he succeeded his father as heir. Piero was already suffering badly from gout just as Cosimo had. Piero's gout was so bad, in fact, that he was known as Piero Il Gottoso (Piero the Gouty). Some people in Florence were not happy with the way in which Piero had automatically taken over power from his father. Florence was, after all, supposed to be a democracy. Diotisalvi Neroni was an extremely influential man in Florence. Before Cosimo died, he told Piero that Neroni was someone who could be trusted completely and who could offer advice about running Florence.

Unfortunately for Piero, Neroni was not the trustworthy person Cosimo believed him to be. Neroni joined forces with Luca Pitti, an extremely powerful and wealthy Florentine banker, and Niccolò Soderini, a devout Republican who believed that the Medicis were dictators and did not truly believe in democracy. The three men formed a conspiracy to topple Piero from power.

Piero discovered the conspiracy. When the plot was exposed, all of the conspirators were exiled except for Luca Pitti, who was allowed to stay in Florence but whose hopes for any sort of power were finished. After the plot's failure, Piero was in a very strong position as undisputed ruler of Florence. However, he could not build upon his success. In 1469, after only five years as ruler, he too died of gout. Many historians think that Piero could have become another great Medici, like Giovanni and Cosimo, if only he had have lived longer. But his successor, his twenty-year-old son

Lorenzo, would turn out to be the greatest Medici of them all.

LORENZO'S EARLY LIFE

Lorenzo de' Medici was born on January 1, 1449. Lorenzo spent most of his early years in the Palazzo Medici, which had been built by his grandfather, Cosimo. All around the palazzo, young Lorenzo was reminded of the exciting times in which he lived. In his bedroom was a painting by Paolo Uccello (1397–1475). In the palazzo's chapel was a fresco by Benozzo Gozzoli (1420–1498), and in the courtyard was Donatello's statue *David*. Lorenzo was constantly exposed to such Renaissance treasures, and his education reflected the new topics of learning from the old worlds.

Lorenzo's teachers were the very best Renaissance scholars in Florence. At the age of nine, Lorenzo was able to memorize and recite poems taught to him by his first tutor, Gentile Becchi. At the age of thirteen, Lorenzo was reading Latin works of poetry, histories, and literature by such people as Ovid and Justinus (third century AD). He learned Greek from Johannis Argyropoulos (circa 1416–1486), who was the head of the Greek

A detail from Benozzo Gozzoli's *Adoration of the Magi*. The great pageant of the three kings was an annual event that took place in Florence on the feast of the Epiphany. This particular detail features a young Lorenzo de' Medici in the center foreground, riding a white horse. The procession features Florentines who took part in the celebration, wearing the red caps like those commonly worn by the Florentine scholars.

department at the city's university, called Florentine Studium. Lorenzo learned poetry from Cristoforo Landino, and philosophy from one of the greatest philosophers of the age, Marsilio Ficino (1433–1499), who had translated Plato into Latin.

Although Lorenzo was dutiful and did very well at his lessons, he wasn't the most enthusiastic pupil. His interest seems to have been as much in play as it was in learning. Lorenzo loved horses and horseback riding. Indeed, breeding horses was one of his favorite hobbies. It was said that Lorenzo was so devoted to his horses that his favorite horse would only be fed by Lorenzo himself. The young boy was also very athletic and enjoyed such sports as tennis, wrestling, and acrobatics. Lorenzo also had a reputation for having a great sense of humor. He was often seen dancing, making jokes, and singing songs at the local festivals.

Physically, Lorenzo was tall and had a strong, athletic body. But he had

Marsilio Ficino, founder of the Platonic Academy, of which Lorenzo would become a member, translated all of Plato's dialogues into Latin. Above is a page of such a translation, dedicated to Lorenzo. Perhaps Ficino's most important contribution was his translation and commentaries in *Platonic Theology*, where he outlines neoplatonism and connects it to Christianity.

some facial features that led some to call him ugly. His nose had flattened nostrils, which caused him to lose his sense of smell, but Lorenzo didn't seem to mind—he said that most smells were unpleasant anyway. Although he was not handsome, his dignity, intelligence, and his love of life made him attractive to many people. Lorenzo's brothers and sisters were more physically beautiful. His brother Giuliano, who was four years younger than Lorenzo, had curly black hair and was considered to be very handsome. Lorenzo's three sisters were named Maria, Nannina, and Bianca.

Lorenzo was very close to his mother, Lucrezia, who became one of his most trusted advisers. She came from a family of rich bankers, the Tornabuoni, and was a very intelligent and attractive woman as well as a very influential and important member of the family. While the Medici men were the powerful figures in the public eye, she offered advice and support from the background. Lucrezia was very religious and made Lorenzo visit the church every day. Although he would never be as strict a Christian as his mother, he also never totally broke away from the church. Lorenzo also learned his love of poetry from his mother. Lucrezia had a reputation as a poet in Florence.

Many historians believe that the biggest influence in Lorenzo's early years came from his father, Piero, and grandfather, Cosimo. Lorenzo was fifteen years old when Cosimo died, so he grew up seeing this great man in action. Piero and Cosimo used every opportunity to introduce Lorenzo to the world of politics, diplomacy, and business—the world that would shape his destiny when the boy grew up. Lorenzo watched as his father and grandfather welcomed ambassadors from foreign lands and learned the art of diplomacy from them. He saw the way in which the elder Medicis dealt with ruthless politicians and the representatives of the pope (who often schemed just as much as the politicians), and how the family's banking business was run. Cosimo and Piero were the perfect teachers to show young Lorenzo the ways of the world, and Lorenzo was an eager and gifted student.

LORENZO GROOMED FOR POWER

When Cosimo died in 1464, and Piero took over as head of the Medici family, Piero's terrible gout meant that he had to rely more and more on Lorenzo to help him. As Piero was often confined to his bed and couldn't travel, he sent Lorenzo on diplomatic missions to represent the Medici family. Lorenzo's first mission was to Pisa to meet Frederico, the son of the king of Naples, who was on his way to Milan to see his elder brother get married. Lorenzo then went on to the marriage ceremony to represent his father. On the way to Milan, Lorenzo visited other Italian states: Bologna, Venice, and Ferrara.

Lorenzo's mission was a great success, especially considering that he was still only a teenager. In 1466, Piero sent his son on the most important mission yet: he sent Lorenzo to Rome to negotiate with Pope Paul II about a contract for the recently discovered alum mines at Tolfa. Alum was a very important mineral used in the Florentine clothing industry because it aided in the dyeing process, turning wool and silk into the most fashionable colors. Lorenzo managed to secure the rights to the alum, which proved very profitable for his family.

Two very important events occurred in 1469. First, Lorenzo married Clarice Orsini in June. Lorenzo was actually in love with another woman named Lucrezia Donati, but she was from a poor family. Lorenzo was a Medici, so he had to marry someone who held equal status in society for the greater good of the Medici family. Clarice's family was from a long line of powerful soldiers who had ties to the pope in Rome. This could prove advantageous for the defense of Florence in times of trouble, and could also strengthen the family's relationship with the pope.

Clarice had bright red hair. She was not thought of as attractive and many believed she knew nothing about the worlds of business, politics, and the arts—things that were such major parts of Lorenzo's life. She also did not share her husband's love of life and fun; some people thought she was somewhat boring. But because the idea of the family was so important for the Medicis, Lorenzo treated Clarice with kindness, even though he may not have been in love with her and had married her only to strengthen the family's position. Clarice and Lorenzo had seven children, three sons and four daughters. It seemed that Lorenzo got along better with his wife as the years passed. When Clarice died in 1488, Lorenzo was said to have shown real grief at her death.

The second major event in Lorenzo's life to occur in 1469 happened on December 2. Piero died. Lorenzo became the undisputed leader of

There are several speculations as to the subject of this famous Sandro Botticelli painting, one of them being that it depicts Lorenzo's wife, Clarice Orsini, circa 1475. Upon choosing Clarice as Lorenzo's bride, his mother, Lucrezia, made a trip to Rome to inspect this heiress to Roman aristocracy, returning to Florence to report that she was indeed a good deal above average. Clarice and Lorenzo were married in San Lorenzo Church and many celebrations and banquets took place around the event.

Florence. All that he had learned from his father and grandfather could now be put into practice. At the age of twenty, Lorenzo had enormous responsibilities and would have to be a special kind of man to rule Florence well at such a young age.

THE PAZZI CONSPIRACY

1
2
4
5

CHAPTER 3

Lorenzo faced trouble in his new position almost immediately after he took power. Piero de' Medici had exiled the conspirators who had risen up against him in 1466, during the Neroni conspiracy. These men thought that since Piero was dead, the time was right to try again. After all, Lorenzo was only a very young man and still very inexperienced at running Florence. In 1470, a band of exiles led by Bernardo Nardi swooped into Prato, a town 30 miles (48 km) from Florence. Their goal was to cause unrest in the small town in the hopes that it would spread to Florence.

The rebels seized the public palace in Prato and captured Cesare Petrucci, a representative from Florence. Nardi addressed the citizens of Prato and told them that the

Medicis were dictators. He urged the citizens to rise up and overthrow Lorenzo. When the people of Prato did not listen to his claims, Nardi changed his tactics, threatening to hang Petrucci from the palace windows. Petrucci asked to address the people as he was their representative. While Petrucci was talking, a young knight gathered a group of volunteers who surrounded the rebels and forced them to surrender.

The rebellion had no chance of success because Lorenzo was popular among the towns surrounding Florence. The Medicis kept villas and country homes outside of Florence. Members of the Medici family went there when they wanted to relax. More important, the villas acted as public relations tools for the family. Because they stayed at the villas, the Medicis became well-known figures by the townspeople. The peasants of the towns grew to like the Medicis; this ensured loyalty, which was of vital importance to the family.

THE VOLTERRAN REVOLT

The Medicis' popularity, however, was tested in 1472 when trouble arose in one of the towns ruled by Florence. The unrest began over an alum-mining contract in the town of Volterra. Again, alum was a

An aerial view of Volterra, Italy, site of the famous revolt that tested the early rule of Lorenzo de' Medici. Volterra had its beginnings in ancient Roman times, and had always been an important mining town. Besides alum, minerals such as iron, silver, and copper were mined there. The Medici Fortress still exists, which Lorenzo ordered to be built after the revolt as a symbol of Florentine rule over the town.

very profitable commodity because of its use in the clothing industry for dyeing wool and silk. Volterra first placed itself under Florentine rule in 1361. Officially, Volterra was a self-governing town, but it owed its safety to Florence. Florence had a permanent representative in Volterra, and the town had to pay a large sum of money each year to Florence for the larger city's protection.

In 1470, a group of businessmen in Volterra acquired a contract for mining alum in the area. Although the Volterran government approved this contract, the people of Volterra were unhappy that the businessmen received the contract to extract a source of wealth from public lands. In June 1471, a new Volterran government seized the mines for itself. As Florence had power over the smaller town, Lorenzo sent a representative to reinstate the group of businessmen. This did not bode well with the Volterrans, and they resisted Lorenzo's attempts to get back the rights to the mines.

This is a page from the secret accounting books of Lorenzo and Cosimo de' Medici. By the time Cosimo the Elder had become Florence's leader, he had taken over most of Florence's thirty-five banks. One lucrative transaction established by the Medici bank was the collecting of 10 percent of people's earnings for the Catholic Church. To not pay would result in excommunication.

Lorenzo was invited to talk to both sides and make a decision as to who owned the rights to the mines. Not surprisingly, Lorenzo decided in favor of the businessmen. It was obviously to Lorenzo's advantage to have the mines in the hands of the businessmen who could be counted on to continue supplying Florence with alum. With the decision made, two of the businessmen returned to the mines with an armed guard and tried to seize back the mines. Their aggressive behavior caused anger among the Volterrans; the situation began to spin out of control. A riot broke out and several people, including one of the businessmen, were murdered. Lorenzo had to make a decision as to how the violence could be stopped. Tragically, he made a mistake.

Lorenzo decided to put down the riots by force. He was angry that his orders had been disobeyed and decided to punish the Volterrans. Lorenzo employed the Duke of Urbino to gather a group of mercenaries. The duke and his 5,000 men massively outnumbered the Volterrans. In less than a month, the Volterrans surrendered. Once in the town, the duke's men went on a rampage of murder, rape, and destruction. Hundreds of people were killed or horribly injured. Lorenzo was appalled at the bloodshed. But while many people did not think that he should be blamed for the actions of the mercenaries, he had forgotten one of the Medici golden rules: cities under your power must be treated well or else they may rise against you.

FRIENDS AND ENEMIES

It wasn't only Florence's local dominions with which Lorenzo had to keep the peace. He also had to try and keep friendly relationships with the other four major powers in Italy: Milan, Naples, Venice, and the pope in Rome. With five independent states in one country, it was in all their interests to get along with each other. Each state was different, however, and as some were very ambitious, this often led to problems. At the start of Lorenzo's rule, relations between Florence, Milan, and Naples were very good. In 1471, Pope Paul II died and a new pope, Sixtus IV (1414–1484), took over. Initially Lorenzo was on good terms with the new pope. But in northern Italy, relations between Milan and Venice were problematic. Lorenzo decided to form an alliance involving Florence, Milan, and Venice to try to bring peace between the two rival states.

Although Rome and Naples were invited to join the alliance, officials there believed that the other three powers were conspiring against them. These two states formed their own alliance, which meant that Italy was now split into two groups that were both suspicious of each other. In 1476, the Duke of Milan was assassinated. His heir was only seven years old—too young to take over leadership. While officials in Milan disputed who should rule while the young duke grew up, Milan grew weak. Lorenzo could no longer rely on his allies in Milan for support. Also, Naples and Rome were now allied, and the good relations between Lorenzo and the new pope were short-lived. Lorenzo and the pope went quickly from being friends to enemies. Florence was surrounded by rival states that were either enemies or were in no position to help Lorenzo if there was trouble, and trouble was approaching.

THE PAZZI CONSPIRACY

The relations between Lorenzo and the new pope, Sixtus IV, started well. However, Sixtus was notorious for giving members of his family positions of power and influence, regardless of their qualifications, or indeed, lack of them. This favoritism pitted the pope and Lorenzo against one another. Sixtus had promised to buy the town of Imola for his nephew, Girolamo Riario. Imola was located in the middle of the trade route between Florence

The Pazzi conspiracy took place in the Cathedral of Santa Maria del Fiore, also known as the Duomo, after the famous dome designed by Brunelleschi. That Easter morning, Giuliano de' Medici, who at the time was suffering from a bad knee, had been helped into the cathedral by his soon-to-be murderers. By affectionately throwing his arms around him, Francesco de' Pazzi was able to feel for any armor Giuliano might have worn, or if he carried a sword.

and Venice. If Imola was in unfriendly hands, it could threaten Florence's trade. Sixtus turned to the Medici bank for a loan with which to buy the town. This put Lorenzo in an awkward position. Obviously, Lorenzo did not want to give Sixtus the money to buy the town for Girolamo. If the pope and his nephew Girolamo controlled the town, they might make trouble along Florence's trade route to Venice. It was as if Lorenzo would be paying the pope to ruin Florence.

Angered at Lorenzo, Sixtus withdrew his account from the Medici bank and transferred it to the Pazzi bank, where he acquired the loan. The Pazzis were a wealthy and respected family in Florence. In many respects, they were allies of the Medicis—one of the Pazzis was married to Lorenzo's sister Bianca. But the Pazzis were also a banking family like the Medicis. This also made the two families business rivals and potential enemies. Having gained the pope's account, and thus a powerful ally, Francesco de' Pazzi began to consider that the time was right to overthrow the Medicis and seize power for his own family. Francesco knew that if he made an attempt to remove Lorenzo without the help of others, the scheme would end in failure. Luckily for Francesco, other powerful people also believed that Lorenzo could be removed.

Francesco de' Pazzi joined forces with Girolamo and Francesco Salviati, who was about to become the new archbishop of Pisa but who really wanted the far more influential position of archbishop of Florence. Most important for the three conspirators, the pope gave his blessing to the planned rebellion. The conspirators knew that although Lorenzo was the ruler of Florence, his brother, Giuliano, was very popular in the city. If they killed only Lorenzo, the Medici supporters would rally around Giuliano. Therefore, the plotters knew that if the plan were to succeed, they had to kill both Lorenzo and Giuliano. The double assassination was planned for Sunday, April 26, 1478, when the Medici brothers would be celebrating Mass in Florence's cathedral.

Francesco de' Pazzi and an associate, Bernardo Bandini Baroncelli, were to be the assassins. While they were killing the brothers in the cathedral, Salviati would march on the Palazzo della Signora and attempt to seize the government. On Sunday, Pazzi and Baroncelli waited for the sanctuary bell to ring— their signal to attack. When the bell rang, they sprang into action. Baroncelli thrust a dagger into Giuliano, shouting, "Take that, traitor!" Pazzi, too, joined the ferocious attack, stabbing Giuliano nineteen times.

Two priests, Maffei and Stefano, were lying in wait to assassinate Lorenzo.

Maffei stabbed Lorenzo in the neck with a dagger. But Lorenzo fought bravely, drawing his sword and wrapping his cape around his arm to act as a shield. He beat off the two murdering priests. Baroncelli moved toward Lorenzo, who made his way to a room in the cathedral where his friends managed to lock the doors behind him. The would-be assassins fled.

Meanwhile, Salviati fared no better in his part of the plot. Salviati and a gang of mercenaries gained entrance to the government building. Nearly fifty loyal Medici supporters soon stormed the building and slaughtered Salviati's hired army. The citizens of Florence were furious that Lorenzo had almost been killed, and their anger turned to riots and murder.

Salviati was hanged, and his body was thrown from the window of the palazzo. Francesco de' Pazzi was also murdered by the mob. Anyone who was involved or even suspected of being involved in the plot was savagely murdered by the mob during the riots, or later by Lorenzo, as he sought revenge for the horrific murder of his beloved brother. Accordingly, revenge for Giuliano's assassination did not end until the 270 conspirators had been

Immediately after his death, a number of portraits were ordered to be painted and placed around Florence of Giuliano de' Medici to serve as both memorials and warnings to any other would-be assassins. It is thought that this portrait of Giuliano, by Sandro Botticelli, served as the prototype. The open window behind him is a symbol of death, alluding to the passage to the afterlife, and his lowered lids are thought to be like that of the death mask.

either killed, exiled, or ruined socially. It would be a brave, or rather a foolish, person who would try to overthrow Lorenzo de' Medici again. Or perhaps a very powerful man could succeed where the plotters had failed—a man like Pope Sixtus IV, the man who had given the conspirators his blessing.

THE BRAVE AND HEROIC DIPLOMAT

Sixtus demanded that Lorenzo come to Rome and apologize for the killing of Salviati, who despite being a would-be murderer was still one of the pope's officials. Lorenzo refused to say he was sorry for the death of the man who had helped kill his brother. In retaliation, the pope excommunicated Lorenzo, banning him from membership in the Catholic Church. This punishment meant that Lorenzo, and in effect all of the citizens of Florence, ran the risk of going to hell when they died because they had disobeyed the pope. Very bravely, Lorenzo offered himself to the pope to save the souls of his people, but the Florentines would not stand for the self-sacrifice of their much-loved leader. Even when Sixtus announced that Rome would declare war on Florence if Lorenzo was not given up, the Florentines still

This painting is titled *Assembly of the Clergy with Pope Sixtus IV*, and was painted by Benozzo Gozzoli. Pope Sixtus was a member of the Franciscan order, which traced its origins to Saint Francis of Assisi. He was elected as pope in 1471, and is considered the first of the Renaissance popes, attracting many painters and sculptors to Rome.

defied him. Sixtus and his ally, King Ferrante of Naples, declared war on Florence in July 1478.

For the city of Florence, the financial burden of the war was great; trade in the city suffered very badly. Lorenzo needed to end the war, but he needed to do it in such a way that he and Florence would not seem defeated. He decided to take personal steps to end the hostilities. Courageously, Lorenzo went straight to his enemy's homeland of Naples and tried to establish peace on behalf of his people with King Ferrante. In a letter addressed to the Florentine Signoria, Lorenzo wrote, "[M]y ardent wish is that either my life or my death should contribute to the good of our city. Should evil befall me, I shall not complain." Lorenzo's brave visit to Naples in 1479 made him a hero in the eyes of the people of Florence. After ten weeks of talks, in which Lorenzo reminded Ferrante that the great rulers of ancient Rome had achieved greatness through peace and not war, the war between Florence and Naples came to an end. Lorenzo had risked his life for his people; his popularity and position as ruler of Florence had never been stronger.

Lorenzo and the Renaissance

Lorenzo de' Medici did not start the Renaissance. The movement had been in full force for years before Lorenzo came to power. But Lorenzo was vitally important in giving direction and purpose to the various aspects of the Renaissance, bringing together artists, scholars, philosophers, and architects. The Medici family had always spent a lot of money on the arts and learning. In his diary, Lorenzo noted that between 1434 and 1471, the family had spent 663,755 florins supporting the arts. To give an idea of exactly how much money this was, a man could live very well in Florence on 200 florins a year. Although this was obviously a lot of money, Lorenzo was happy to carry on the family tradition of patronizing learning and the arts.

Cosimo de' Medici had built Europe's first public library. Lorenzo shared his grandfather's love of books and collected manuscripts from all over the world. In one year alone, Lorenzo spent 30,000 florins on manuscripts. He collected some of the best works to have come from the classical civilizations. In 1492, for example, 200 ancient Greek manuscripts, almost half of which had never been read in Italy before, were brought back to Florence from the monastery at Mount Athos in Greece. Lorenzo's manuscripts included works by the famous mathematician Archimedes (circa 287–212 BC), the writings of such men as Homer (ninth century BC) and Cicero (106–43 BC), as well as books that described the philosophy of Plato and ideas about architecture.

Cosimo de' Medici, Lorenzo's grandfather, had a great desire to open public libraries. The first such library was part of the Dominican monastery of San Marco in Florence. Designed by Michelozzo, it was modeled after the Roman style. Manuscripts, mostly from the collection of the famous humanist Niccolò Niccoli, were chained to benches placed in rows.

ϹΟΒΟϹΩ ΤΙΒΛΥΚΟ ϹΛΝΗΡ
ΕΝΕ ΜΕΛΛΜΛΝ
ΛΟΥϹΛΤΕΤΩΛ ΛΡΛΥΠΟΥΟ
ΟΧΟΝΛΛΕΡΚΙ ΔΟΜΕ ΛΕϹϹ
ΡΟΟϹΕΡΧ Ν ΤΙΡΙϹΛΥΗ
ΤΕΛΕΙϹΙΟΥ
ΥΤΟΝΕϹΘ
ΥΛΕϹ
ϹΕΛ ΛΡΒΟΥϹ
ϹΗ
ΧΙ ΕΤϹ

ΕΡΙ ΕΓΕΝ

ΛΕΒΙΕΙ
ΓΧΕΝΟΥΛϹ
ΘΡΛϹΤΥΜ ΛΗϹ
ϹΟΥΚΙΝ
ΤΙΝΕϹΙ
ΤΟΠΟΛΛΛϹΙΙ
ΤΡΙΧΛϹϹ ΤΥΡΙΚ ΛΩΝ
ΥΤΛΙΗ ΟΒΛΛΩΝ
ΙϹΟΡΛΟϹΥΜΗΛΙ
ϹΥΕΤΕΝ ΟΝΤΡϹ
ΛΙΛΟΛΛΥϹΛΝ
ΛΚΟΙΠϹ
ΙΟΘΥΓΑΤΡΩΝ
ΥΡΥΟΔΕΙΝϹ
ΘΡΛΛΜΘΟΛΛΝΛΡϹ
ΛΟϹΤΕΛΘΥΜΟϹ
ΡΙΛΛΜΙΝΟΝ

ΤΑΙ ΤΛΚ
ΔΙΤ ΤΥΧΛΙϹ
ΚΛΙΕΔϹΠΙϹΧ ϹΙ Ε ΩΝ
ΛΕΙΒΕΝΕΟΙΛΕΙ ΛΛΥΤΟΝΕΧΟ
ΛΥΤΙΡΕΠΕΙΚΑΤΛΙΡΙΕϹΚΛΝΚΙ
ΛΛΟΝΤΛΡΛΤΛΛΛΑΚΙΙΙϹΟ
ΩΝΔΛΚΡΟΠΟΡΟΥϹΟΒΕΛ
ΛΕΤΙΛΕΜΑΧΟΝΛΟΥϹΕ
ΛΟΤΙΙΠΟΥΙΛΤΙ
ΡΕΠΕΙΛΥϹϹΝΤϹΚΙΙΕΧ
Ι ΔΕΙΝΦΛΡΟϹΚΛΛΟΝΒΛΙ
ΡϹΑΛΙΝΘΟΥΒΗΔΕΛΛϹΛΘ
ΛΡΔΟΓΕΝΕϹΤΟΒΙΩΝΚΑΤΛΡΟ
ΟΙΛΕΤΕΙΩΠΠΗϹΙΝΚΡΕΥΠΕ
ΛΝΝΥΝΘϹΧΟΜΕΝΟΙΕΠΙΛΛ
ΟΙΝΟΝΕΝΟΙΝΟΧΟϹΟΥΝΤϹϹΕΝ
ΛΥΤΙΡΕΠΙΠΟϹΙΟϹΚΙΙΕΛΗΤΥ
ΤΟΙϹΙΔΕΙΙΥΑΙΙΝΗΙΡΧΕΓϹΕΗ
ΠΙΛΕϹΕΜΟΙΛΙΓΕΠΛϹΛΙΧΥΙΙ
ΖΕΥΧΛΘΥΦΛΡΜΑΤΑΓΟΝΤΕϹΟΙΝΑΤΙ
ΟϹϹΕΦΛϢΟΙΔΛΡΛΤΟΥΜΛΛΛΙΕΝΙ
ΚΑΡΠΛΛΜΙΙϹΛΕΖΕΥΞΛΝΥΦΡΛΙ
ΛΝΔΕΓΥΙΙΤΑΜΙΗϹΙΤΟΝΚΛΙΟΙ
ΟΥΛΤΕΟ ΛΕΛΟΥϹΙΔΙΟΤΡΕΦΕϹ
ΛΝ ΛΚΛΙΠΛΕΜΑΧΟϹΠΕΡΙ ΛΛ
ΠΡΑΛΛΑΝΕϹΤΟΡΙΛΗϹΠ ΠΙϹΤ
ΕϹΛΙΦΡΟΝΛΛΝϹΒΛΙΝϹΚΛΙΦΙΝΙ
ΛΜΑϹΤΙϹΕΝΔΕΧΛΛΝΤΩΛΟΥΚϹ
ΘϹΤΕΛ ΘΝΛΙΠΕΠΙΝΛΕΠΥΛΟΥ
ΛΟ ΤΙΛΗΜΕΡΙΟΙϹΕΙΟΝΧΥΓΟΝ
ΘΗΡΛϹΛΙΚΟΝΤΟΛΙΟΚΛΗΟϹΤΙ
ϹΟΡΠΙΛΟΧΡΙϹΤΟΝΛΛΦΕΙΟϹ
ΦΛΔΕΝΥΚΤΛΕϹΛΝΟΛΕΤΟΕΓΙ
ΗΜΟϹΔΗΡΙΓΕΝΕΙΑΦΛΝΗΡΟΛΔ
ΙΠΠΟΥϹΤΕΖΕΥΓΝΥΝΤΙΝΛΛΟΚΛ

These are fragments of a papyrus copy of the *Odyssey* (from the first century BC) by Homer. Homer's poem tells the story of Odysseus's return home after the Trojan War. Odysseus was known for his great talent for trickery. For example, it was his idea to fill a giant wooden horse with Greek soldiers, which was then allowed inside Troy's gates by Trojans who believed it was a gift. The humanists of Lorenzo's time took great interest in these stories because they examined the value of a human life and what a person should try to achieve in his or her lifetime.

Lorenzo also donated a lot of money to the University of Florence. The university was the perfect model of a Renaissance school and had the reputation of being the only college in Europe where the Greek language was taught properly. The printing press had recently been invented and two teachers from the university, Demetrius Chalcondylas (1424–1511) and Demetrius Cretensis, produced the first printed edition of the works of Homer in 1488. Students from all over Europe came to Florence to study at this renowned place of learning. One such student was Thomas Linacre, who became the personal doctor of the great English king Henry VIII (1491–1547).

Although Lorenzo's main interests were education and ancient manuscripts, he was also a patron to the talented artists who were coming to the fore in this exciting atmosphere. Lorenzo was directly responsible for starting the careers of some of the world's most brilliant artists. He also patronized such people as sculptor and painter Andrea del Verrocchio (1435–1488), who taught Leonardo da Vinci (1452–1519), considered by many people as the greatest artist of all time. Even when Lorenzo did not directly commission the artists, he always tried to make sure that promising people were employed by other rich and influential patrons. Lorenzo found work in other cities in Italy for artists including painter Filippo Lippi (circa 1457–1504) and sculptor Giuliano da Maiano (1432–1490).

Lorenzo genuinely loved the arts, but there were often business reasons behind his patronage. Lorenzo hired some French musicians to perform in Florence. Although he may have enjoyed the music of the Frenchmen, the fact that Lorenzo had hired people from such a powerful country as France no doubt increased his reputation in that country and also improved relations with this important neighbor. Lorenzo's organist, Squarcialupi, had an international reputation, which drew people from all over Europe to Florence to hear him play. By promoting Squarcialupi, Lorenzo brought more people into Florence. These tourists, in turn, spent their money in the city during their stay, helping the businesses of Lorenzo's city.

BOTTICELLI

Lorenzo was totally devoted to the works of artist Sandro Botticelli, who had studied with artist Filippo Lippi. Botticelli's growing reputation as a

This is one of several studies by Andrea del Verrocchio, titled *Head of a Girl*, circa 1475. Verrocchio rose to prominence in Florence only after the death of Donatello, who had previously been the favorite artist of the Medicis. By the late fifteenth century, his Florentine studio was the center of the city's art scene, attracting Leonardo da Vinci, and Raphael's teacher, Perugino.

brilliant painter brought him to the attention of Lorenzo. Botticelli soon became Lorenzo's "official" artist. In 1475, Botticelli produced *Adoration of the Magi*, featuring the three generations of Medicis portrayed to show their greatness: Cosimo is the main figure, with his son Piero, and his grandsons Lorenzo and Giuliano represented in the foreground of the picture. Botticelli painted himself into the far right of the picture, which many historians think is meant to show his support for the family and their ideals.

Botticelli produced several other paintings for Lorenzo, including a number of portraits of Giuliano, Lorenzo's murdered brother. After Lorenzo's triumphant return from Naples after ending the war, Botticelli painted *Pallas and the Centaur* for Lorenzo, which symbolized peace over force. But Botticelli's most famous painting, the *Birth of Venus*, became a symbol to Lorenzo. To Lorenzo and the other neoplatonists, the goddess Venus was the perfect representation of the united philosophy of Christianity with the new learning put into place by the Renaissance. She was a symbol of innocence and new birth.

This is Sandro Botticelli's *Adoration of the Magi*, circa 1475. In the Bible, at the time of Christ's birth, three kings (often referred to as the magi) followed a star that led them to the newborn savior. They brought him gifts of gold, frankincense, and myrrh. This theme was painted in the fifteenth century with great frequency, due to the importance of various brotherhoods or fraternities, common in Florentine life at the time, one such being the Brotherhood of the Magi.

MICHELANGELO

Michelangelo was another great artist whom Lorenzo sponsored. In 1488, Lorenzo set up a school for talented sculptors in Florence. He believed that although there were many great painters in the city, there were not enough brilliant sculptors. Lorenzo used the Medici gardens, a small private park between the Palazzo Medici and the monastery of San Marco, as the venue for this new school. The master of the school was Bertoldo di Giovanni, a former pupil of Cosimo de' Medici's favorite sculptor, Donatello. Lorenzo gave the school many paintings, busts, and statues so that the students could copy them and improve their skills.

According to legend, one day Michelangelo was making a copy of one of these ancient pieces, the

Michelangelo's *David* was commissioned in 1501 to be a symbol of the power and determination of the new Florentine republic after the Medicis were temporarily ousted from power. Michelangelo chose to sculpt the biblical hero in the tense moment before battle with the giant Goliath.

head of a fawn. Lorenzo passed by and was amazed at the skill of the young boy, so he decided to promote this brilliant artist. Lorenzo moved Michelangelo into his own home, the Palazzo Medici, where Michelangelo spent the next four years. Lorenzo became so fond of the young sculptor that he came to look upon the boy as his own son. Michelangelo always ate at Lorenzo's table, along with Lorenzo's own sons and any other important people who were visiting. This was a great honor for Michelangelo. Later, Michelangelo created *David*, one of the greatest sculptures the world has ever seen. Michelangelo also produced one of the world's most famous paintings—his design on the ceiling of the Sistine Chapel.

Because Lorenzo didn't commission many pieces himself, some historians claim that his reputation as a major influence on the art of the Renaissance has been exaggerated. But even though Lorenzo did not commission many artists himself, he found them work with other patrons. Lorenzo's patronage of Botticelli and Michelangelo alone is tribute to the influence he had on the Renaissance and the arts in general. He believed that art should be enjoyed simply because it is beautiful. As Lorenzo instructed his artists to produce works with simple beauty in mind, he can be truly looked upon as a driving force of the Renaissance.

THE RENAISSANCE MAN

Lorenzo had been educated by some of the best Renaissance scholars, so he cared deeply about the ideals of this rebirth of knowledge. Lorenzo was one of the most important men in Florence, so it was natural that other Renaissance enthusiasts would look to him for leadership. A group of brilliant men began to gather around Lorenzo to discuss philosophy, poetry, and the Renaissance in general. It was an informal group rather than a proper organization, what is called a think tank today. The group became known as the Platonic Academy. Its members included politicians, doctors, artists, musicians, and lawyers who met to discuss how the philosophy of Plato could enhance humankind.

The Platonic Academy met whenever possible at various locations, often at Lorenzo's country villas in Fiesole and Careggi, two towns that surrounded Florence. It was always sure to meet on one special day, November 7, the date of Plato's birth, when a big banquet was held in the philosopher's honor. The academy became very influential in Italy, and indeed its ideas were debated in many parts of Europe. When the leaders of Naples and Milan wanted to build new palaces, they turned to Lorenzo and his friends for advice on designs. A competition was held to design a new look for Florence's cathedral. Many members of the academy, including Botticelli and Verrocchio, were among the twenty-eight entrants. Even Lorenzo submitted a design.

Perhaps the most brilliant member of the Platonic Academy was a handsome young man with long golden hair named Giovanni Pico della Mirandola (1463–1494). Pico had studied at four universities by the time he was eighteen, and it was said that he could speak twenty-two different languages. Pico also studied Hebrew, and it was through his interest that many more people began to look again at ancient Hebrew thought. Sometimes, however, Pico's love for learning got him into trouble. In 1486, he went to Rome where he announced that he would debate 900 different topics—ethics, theology, mathematics, among various others—with anyone who wanted to challenge him. Pope Innocent VIII (1432–1492), however, was not happy with some of the topics and accused Pico of heresy, or going against God. Scared for his life, Pico fled to France, where he was arrested. Luckily, Lorenzo arranged to have Pico set free.

Here, the celebration of Plato's birthday on November 7, 1474, at Lorenzo de' Medici's villa in Careggi is depicted later by nineteenth-century artist Luigi Mussini. It is believed that Plato died on his birthday at age eighty-one after enjoying a large banquet in his honor. The ancient Platonists always celebrated this date. Twelve hundred years later in Florence, Lorenzo restored the banquet in honor of the great philosopher.

Another member of the Platonic Academy was poet Angelo Poliziano (1454–1494). He was five years younger than Lorenzo; the two men had met when Poliziano had translated Homer's *The Iliad* into Latin. Lorenzo invited him to live at the Palazzo Medici where they became best friends. Later Poliziano became the teacher of Lorenzo's children. Poliziano was also made professor of Latin and Greek at the University of Florence. His poetry was based on the styles of the ancient Greek and Roman poets. In fact, he was so obsessed with the languages of the ancient civilizations that he not only spoke Greek and Latin, but it was said that he thought in these languages as well. He also wrote *Orfeo*, which was the first Italian operatic drama.

LORENZO THE POET

Though Lorenzo was always busy running Florence, and also the Medici bank, he was often heard saying how he wished he could escape to the country where he could spend time with his friends and indulge in one of his favorite pastimes, reading and writing poetry. Lorenzo loved to relax by writing poems and had a reputation as being a very good poet. But what was truly remarkable about Lorenzo's poetry was the language in which it was written. At that time, Latin was considered a universal language in Europe. Although it was the language used by the ancient Romans, it was also the language in which all government, church, and scholarly works were written during the Renaissance period. Lorenzo did not write his poetry in Latin. Instead, he chose to write in the vernacular, or the normal spoken form of the language, which was Tuscan Italian. Lorenzo wanted to write poetry in a language that could be understood by his people—all people, not just the scholarly elite.

Considered to be one of Lorenzo's finest poems, *Ambra* was written to celebrate the Medici's country villa at Poggio a Caiano. This theme of commemorating the beauty of the land around Florence and the nature that it contained is often featured in Lorenzo's poems. In *Ambra*, Lorenzo describes how the cranes fly past the villa during the wintertime:

> Marking the tracts of air,
> The clamorous cranes wheel their
>   due flight,
> In varied lines described;
> And each with outstretched neck his
>   rank maintains
> In marshalled order through the
>   ethereal void.

Some of Lorenzo's most memorable lines come from *Giovinezza*, a song written about the Roman gods Bacchus and Ariadne. Also featured in the song is King Midas, whom Lorenzo believes has wasted his life and found no pleasure in any of his many years. In the following excerpt, Lorenzo reminds us that we are young only once and that we should enjoy this part of our lives, as we never know what the future holds:

> Listen well to what we're saying;
> Of tomorrow we have no care!

The late-nineteenth-century Italian painter Tito Lessi (1858–1917) depicted a Florentine apprentice working the printing press in the late fifteenth century. When news of the printing press that had been invented in Mainz, Germany, reached Florence in the mid-1450s, many Florentine scholars considered it to be a crude, barbaric process. Lorenzo traditionally hired numerous scribes and illustrators to replicate manuscripts. Finally, the printing press was established in Florence in 1477.

Young and old together playing,
Boys and girls be blithe of air!
Every sorry thought forswear!
Keep perpetual holiday–
Youth and maids, enjoy today;
Nought ye know about tomorrow.

Lorenzo also wrote many beautiful sonnets. The following was written in honor of his brother Giuliano's lover, Simonetta Vespucci, who had recently died. In the sonnet, Lorenzo and a friend are walking together and see a bright star in the sky. He wonders if the brilliance of the star is because Simonetta's bright eyes have merged with the star in heaven:

O bright star, whose rays rob all
  neighboring stars of their light,
Why do you shine with such
  unwonted splendor,
Why do you rival even great Phoebus?
Perhaps it is because you have taken
  to yourself those beauteous eyes
  of which cruel death had presumed
  to rob us;
Adorned with their light you can challenge
  the sun's chariot.

Lorenzo also wrote a play called *La rappresentazione di San Giovanni e Paolo* (Representations of Saints John and Paul), which was performed in 1489 by a group of young boys from the Company of St. John the Evangelist. One of Lorenzo's sons, Giuliano, acted in the play. According to legend, Lorenzo also took part in the play, portraying emperors Constantine and Julian. The story is about Emperor Constantine and how he gave up his throne to evil successors who did not tolerate anyone who disagreed with them. Eventually, Constantine's successors lost all their power.

In the part of the play where Constantine retires and gives his crown to his successor, the character's words seem to be those of Lorenzo himself, expressing his ideas on how the perfect ruler should lead his people. Lorenzo uses this character to confide how the role of leader may seem to be glamorous, but how it often brings much heartache. He describes how leaders should always try to rule for the good of the people as a whole and not just for selfish reasons. Leaders are role models and should always set a good example. If people look up to their leaders, and if the leaders act badly, the people may do so as well. Although this was stated in the imaginary world of a play, it seems Lorenzo truly meant the words he wrote for Constantine, and always tried to lead Florence by these ideals.

LORENZO THE MAGNIFICENT

When Lorenzo came back from Naples in 1479, after meeting with King Ferrante to end the war, he was in a very strong position. Lorenzo's brave actions had only increased the love and affection that the people of Florence felt for him. He also gained respect from others, making the people look at him as the peace-keeper of Italy. At this time, Lorenzo came to be called *il Magnifico*, "the Magnificent." When we look at his actions after the Pazzi conspiracy and the war, it becomes obvious that he truly deserved this title. But Lorenzo still had to work hard to be considered magnificent. Although there was peace, the other Italian states were hardly very friendly to each other, and the pope remained a powerful enemy.

On August 6, 1480, the Ottoman Turks invaded Italy. Turkish ships attacked Otranto and besieged the city. This invasion was totally and utterly unexpected. Turkish forces had recently attacked the city of Rhodes in Greece, but taking the city proved hard for the Turks, so they gave up the siege. Perhaps wanting to restore some pride after their defeat at Rhodes, the Turks decided to invade while sailing close to the Italian shores. This was a large-scale invasion with 7,000 men storming into the city; more Turks were preparing to attack Albania. Rumors spread that the Turks were ready to march on Rome, which would have had serious consequences for the whole of Italy.

The Turkish invasion put Pope Sixtus IV in a difficult position. Throughout his career, he seemed to enjoy stirring up trouble between the rival Italian states. Now, if he was not to be overthrown by the invading Turks, he had to call on all of Italy to pull together to defeat the foreign enemy. One of the people he would have to seek help from was Lorenzo.

After the Pazzi conspiracy, Sixtus had excommunicated Lorenzo, and both men remained enemies. Lorenzo did not want to apologize to the pope because he felt he had done nothing wrong. As the pope wouldn't apologize either, there was a stalemate between the two men. It was in Lorenzo's

The city-state of Venice had a powerful navy, which, during the fifteenth century, fought a series of wars with the Turks who were always looking to expand the Ottoman Empire over control of the Mediterranean Sea. The manuscript above, from this time, documents such an event. Peace was finally made between the Venetians and Turks in 1479, before the Turks' invasion of Otranto the next year.

best interests, and that of Florence, to make amends with the pope. Sixtus was such a powerful figure and, as head of the church, was an important symbol to the Catholic religion. The Turkish invasion meant that both had to put their differences aside for the greater good.

The Turkish invasion offered a perfect opportunity for Lorenzo to approach the pope. Some people thought that the situation was rather suspicious. They believed that Lorenzo might have arranged the invasion. This would give him an opportunity to make friends with the pope again. Others thought this idea was ridiculous. But whatever the truth was, Lorenzo and Sixtus put aside their differences to vanquish the enemy Turks. The pope forgave Lorenzo and Florence, and the Turks were defeated in 1481. Even though they were officially allies again, Lorenzo and the pope still distrusted each other. There was a real possibility that they would soon be enemies once more and that Lorenzo would once again be called upon to make peace.

THE TROUBLESOME POPE

Sixtus IV once again involved Italy in a war. The pope's nephew, Girolamo Riario, who had been part of the Pazzi conspiracy, still wanted to be a powerful figure in Italy. With the backing of his uncle, Girolamo was always looking for ways to make this happen. In May 1482, Girolamo and Sixtus joined forces with the powerful state of Venice and declared war against Duke Ercole of Ferrara. Once more, the peace of Italy was shattered and the various states had to decide which side to back and with whom to make alliances.

Milan and Naples joined forces with Florence and sent troops to attack Rome and Venice. But Lorenzo didn't want to attack his neighbors because his greatest wish was for peace in Italy. He secretly pushed to bring the war to an end. Sixtus realized that because Venice was so powerful, it might decide to keep all of the lands of Ferrara for itself. This worry, combined with Lorenzo's peace negotiations, prompted Sixtus to declare war on his former ally and forge an alliance with Milan, Naples, and Florence.

This was a good alliance for Italy. Although Venice was powerful on its own, it was not as powerful as the other states combined. But Italy was still at war and once again it was Lorenzo who made the effort to bring peace. The Venetians realized that they had no hope of defeating the combined states. A meeting was called at Bagnolo

Leonardo da Vinci's *Bust of a Warrior in Profile*, circa 1475 to 1480, was drawn with a sharp metal pen. This type of art is known as silverpoint. Many young, serious apprentice artists worked this way, which required immense precision and control. Most likely, da Vinci was studying a work of his master Andrea del Verrocchio. Perhaps it was Verrocchio's portrait of Alexander the Great, the great leader of the Greeks, which Lorenzo de' Medici then sent as a gift to the king of Hungary.

in August 1484, and peace was declared. The day after the peace treaty was signed, Pope Sixtus IV died. Some people said he died because he no longer wanted to live in a world where he couldn't make war.

LORENZO THE PEACEMAKER

With Sixtus IV's death, a new pope, Innocent VIII, was elected. Lorenzo did not want a repeat of his bad relations with the pope, so he immediately set about trying to get on friendly terms with Innocent. Luckily for Lorenzo, the new pope wasn't a troublemaker like Sixtus. But Lorenzo still felt that he should do everything in his power to make Innocent an ally. Lorenzo sent agents to find out what Innocent liked and then sent him presents of these things. These included casks of the pope's favorite wine and gifts of ortolans, which the pope enjoyed eating. Ortolans are very small birds, which were cooked and eaten whole. They were considered a great delicacy. This campaign of getting on the good side of the new pope worked, and Innocent came to like and respect Lorenzo. Lorenzo further strengthened this new alliance when he supported the marriage of his daughter Maddelana to the pope's son.

Innocent came to trust Lorenzo and to look to him for advice. However, the peace in Italy was still fragile and trouble arose again in 1485. Innocent wanted the people of Naples to pay taxes to Rome. Also, the feudal barons in Naples were on the verge of revolt against their leader, King Ferrante. The pope used this unrest to his advantage and declared war on Naples. The steps Lorenzo had taken to make the new pope an ally seemed to have worked because it was

INNOCENTIVS·VIII·PAPA·GENVENSIS·
fu fatto del 1484 uise ani 7 mesi o giorni 11

Pope Innocent VIII came to trust Lorenzo so much that one frustrated papal ambassador to another city-state complained that the genial, easygoing pope saw everything through the eyes of Lorenzo de' Medici.

Lorenzo who brought both sides to the table and persuaded them to make peace in 1486.

History has shown that Lorenzo brought peace to Italy many times during this period of civil unrest. Among so many rulers who seemed determined to make war whenever they could, Lorenzo de' Medici alone was the man who tried everything in his power to make peace. Lorenzo strove to keep the various states of Italy in alliance, which he hoped would stop one state becoming more powerful than the others. This form of diplomacy is called the balance of power, and has been used as a strategy in international affairs throughout history. Lorenzo had a huge influence in keeping the peace in Italy. For this alone, one could say that Lorenzo de' Medici most certainly deserves the title of "magnificent."

THE LAST YEARS

Lorenzo was a brilliant politician, diplomat, and patron of the arts. There was one area, however, in which Lorenzo was not as accomplished—running the family bank. Because he was involved in so many other tasks, Lorenzo did not always have the time to attend to business. The bank was so large that it was impossible for one man to run it on his own. Lorenzo was more interested in politics and the arts than in banking, so he often left the running of the bank to his managers. In some cases, these people abused the trust Lorenzo had given them. Some of these Medici bank managers stole money from the bank. Others lent money to people who could not pay back their loans, resulting in a loss of bank funds. The actions of these bad managers meant that the Medici banks had to be sold.

It must be stated, however, that Lorenzo often used money that was not his to spend. Because he was not very good with his financial affairs, he was often short of money. To help himself out of financial difficulties, he took money that didn't belong to him from places such as the treasury of Florence. Once, he took 55,000 florins from a trust fund set up for two of his young cousins. When the boys came of age to use the fund, there was no money left. Instead of paying them back the money, which he could not do, Lorenzo gave them various houses and villas. This still did not add up to the amount that he had taken from the fund.

GIROLAMO SAVONAROLA

Although people in Italy and throughout Europe viewed Lorenzo as a great leader, there were some who did not appreciate the way he ran Florence.

Giralomo Savonarola is depicted here preaching to a Florentine crowd. Even though there were those Florentine citizens who rejected his zealousness, many more became his followers, participating in the burning of books, artwork, jewelry, and any other items condemned as vulgar and ungodly. Finally, even these followers began to tire of Savonarola, and a riot commenced during his Ascension Day sermon. Taverns reopened and men began to gamble freely. Savonarola was finally burned at the stake on May 23, 1498.

Girolamo Savonarola (1452–1498), a monk from Venice, became Lorenzo's biggest critic during the last years of his reign. Pico della Mirandola, from the Platonic Academy, had seen Savonarola in Venice, where he was preaching against the corruption of the church in Rome. Pico persuaded Lorenzo to bring the monk to Florence. Unfortunately for Lorenzo, Savonarola also had another cause that he wanted to tell people about.

Savonarola arrived in Florence around 1485, and immediately began to criticize, in very violent and terrifying words, the lifestyle and philosophy of the people of Florence. The monk believed that the Renaissance was evil because it stressed the importance of ancient Greece and Rome. Savonarola claimed that the Florentines were turning away from God. He preached that if the Florentines did not return to God, terrifying plagues and famine would hit the city. He said that those who did not do as he commanded would die, spending

Poggio a Caiano was Lorenzo's favorite villa. He kept an array of exotic animals on the grounds, including a giraffe that had been a gift from the sultan of Babylon. He would spend his last days at the beloved villa, often appearing in the window to passersby in an effort to dispel the rumor he was dying.

eternity in hell. Thousands of people came to hear Savonarola preach, and many of them were frightened by what he had to say. They began to question the philosophy of the Renaissance and, indeed, of Lorenzo himself.

Many of the great Renaissance thinkers in Florence began also to question their belief in the rebirth of learning. Pico, Poliziano, and Botticelli all became followers of Savonarola. Accusations that Lorenzo was wasting public money on the arts, combined with the frightening words that the monk used, made many believe that the dream of an enlightened Florence was over. As a result, Lorenzo was seen less and less in public, and he began to seek refuge from the crisis at his country villas. There Lorenzo read, took pleasure in the beauty of the countryside, sought comfort among his friends and family, and tried to forget the troubles that were brewing in the city.

As his father and grandfather had, Lorenzo suffered from gout. During the Savonarola crisis, the disease hit him very badly. Lorenzo knew that he was dying. To ensure the Medici family would continue to rule Florence after his death, Lorenzo began to plan for his children's futures. He arranged marriages for his daughters to the sons of other important families in Florence. Lorenzo knew that after his death, his eldest son, Piero (1471–1503), would take over leadership of Florence. But Piero was not a great man; he was known as being arrogant, undisciplined, and untalented. Whereas Lorenzo was called the Magnificent, Piero was known as the Unfortunate. Lorenzo believed that Piero would be a

Piero di Lorenzo de' Medici was said to have inherited his father's ruthlessness but lacked his tact. As a child, he seems to have been spoiled. In one letter to his father, he expresses his impatience to own the best sporting dog. After he received the dog he wanted a pony, complaining he was being ridiculed for not having one. By the time he inherited his father's reign, he seemed to feel secure in its permanency, and mostly avoided public affairs and business, leaving the duties to his secretary.

weak leader, so he arranged for his fourteen-year-old son, Giovanni, to become a cardinal with the church. This meant that once Piero took power, he would have an ally in his relations with the pope.

In the spring of 1492, Lorenzo was taken to the villa at Careggi to die. Savonarola visited Lorenzo. Despite being Lorenzo's enemy, the monk absolved Lorenzo of his sins—a custom performed by an official of the Catholic Church when someone is about to die. Lorenzo died on Sunday evening, April 8, 1492. He was buried with his brother, Giuliano, in the tomb of the Medici chapel at San Lorenzo Church. Although Lorenzo had requested a small funeral, many Florentines wanted to honor their beloved leader. Much of Florence's population attended the service. Poliziano, Lorenzo's best friend, wrote these words:

> O That my head were
> waters, and my eyes
> a fount of tears,
> that I might weep by day
> and weep by night!

After Lorenzo's death, his son Piero became ruler of Florence. But it did not take long for all of Lorenzo's

The tomb of Lorenzo de' Medici *(left)* is found in the Medici Chapel in San Lorenzo Church in Florence. The chapel and tomb were designed by Michelangelo and completed in 1534. The tomb features a statue of Lorenzo portrayed as a soldier, with his eyes cast downward, deep in thought. Underneath him lie figures representing dawn and dusk.

work in securing peace in Italy to unravel. In 1494, France invaded Italy and threatened Florence. In negotiations with the French, Piero surrendered. Outraged at this, the Florentine government expelled Piero. The unthinkable had happened: the Medicis no longer ruled Florence. Nearly eighteen years later, however, the Medicis did regain power in Florence. In 1512

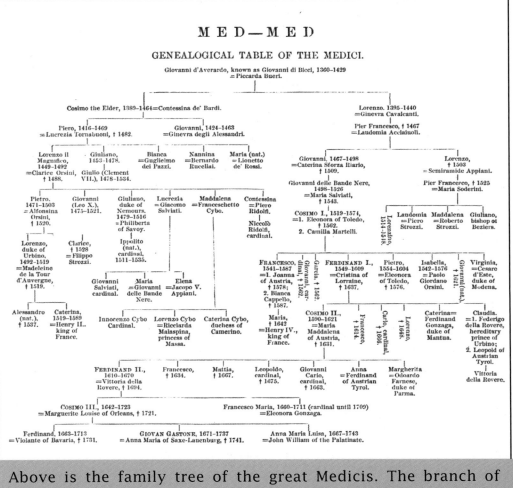

GENEALOGICAL TABLE OF THE MEDICI.

Giovanni d'Averardo, known as Giovanni di Bici, 1360-1429
= Piccarda Bueri.

Cosimo the Elder, 1389-1464=Contessina de' Bardi.

Lorenzo, 1395-1440
=Ginevra Cavalcanti.

Piero, 1416-1469
=Lucrezia Tornabuoni, † 1482.

Giovanni, 1424-1463
=Ginevra degli Alessandri.

Pier Francesco, † 1467
=Laudomia Acciaiuoli.

Lorenzo il Magnifico, 1449-1492
=Clarice Orsini, † 1488.

Giuliano, 1453-1478.

Bianca
=Guglielmo dei Pazzi.

Nannina
=Bernardo Rucellai.

Maria (nat.)
=Lionetto de' Rossi.

Giovanni, 1467-1498
=Caterina Sforza Riario, † 1509.

Lorenzo,
=Semiramide Appiani.

Giuliano, Giulio (Clement VII.), 1478-1534.

Giovanni delle Bande Nere, 1498-1526
=Maria Salviati, † 1543.

Pier Francesco, † 1525
=Maria Soderini.

Pietro, 1471-1503
=Alfonsina Orsini, † 1520.

Giovanni (Leo X.), 1475-1521.

Giuliano, duke of Nemours, 1479-1516
=Philiberta of Savoy.

Lucrezia
=Giacomo Salviati.

Maddalena
=Franceschetto Cybo.

Contessina
=Piero Ridolfi.

Niccolò Ridolfi, cardinal.

COSIMO I., 1519-1574,
=1. Eleonora of Toledo, † 1562.
2. Camilla Martelli.

Lorenzino, 1514-1548.

Laudomia
=Piero Strozzi.

Maddalena
=Roberto Strozzi.

Giuliano, bishop of Beziers.

Lorenzo, duke of Urbino, 1492-1519
=Madeleine de la Tour d'Auvergne, † 1519.

Clarice, † 1528
=Filippo Strozzi.

Ippolito (nat.), cardinal, 1511-1535.

FRANCESCO, 1541-1587
=1. Joanna of Austria, † 1578;
2. Bianca Cappello, † 1587.

Garzia, † 1562.

Giovanni, cardinal, † 1562.

FERDINAND I., 1549-1609
=Cristina of Lorraine, † 1637.

Pietro, 1554-1604
=Eleonora of Toledo, † 1576.

Isabella, 1542-1576
=Paolo Giordano Orsini.

Virginia,
=Cesare d'Este, duke of Modena.

Giovanni (nat.), † 1621.

Giovanni Salviati, cardinal.

Maria
=Giovanni delle Bande Nere.

Elena
=Jacopo V. Appiani.

Alessandro (nat.), † 1537.

Caterina, 1519-1589
=Henry II., king of France.

Innocenzo Cybo Cardinal.

Lorenzo Cybo
=Ricciarda Malaspina, princess of Massa.

Caterina Cybo, duchess of Camerino.

Maria, † 1642
=Henry IV., king of France.

COSIMO II., 1590-1621
=Maria Maddalena of Austria, † 1631.

Francesco, † 1614.

Carlo, cardinal, † 1666.

Lorenzo, † 1648.

Caterina=Ferdinand Gonzaga, duke of Mantua.

Claudia,
=1. Federigo della Rovere, hereditary prince of Urbino;
2. Leopold of Austrian Tyrol.

Vittoria della Rovere.

FERDINAND II., 1610-1670
=Vittoria della Rovere, † 1694.

Francesco, † 1634.

Mattia, † 1667.

Leopoldo, cardinal, † 1675.

Giovanni Carlo, cardinal, † 1663.

Anna
=Ferdinand of Austrian Tyrol.

Margherita
=Odoardo Farnese, duke of Parma.

COSIMO III., 1642-1723
=Marguerite Louise of Orleans, † 1721.

Francesco Maria, 1660-1711 (cardinal until 1709)
=Eleonora Gonzaga.

Ferdinand, 1663-1713
=Violante of Bavaria, † 1731.

GIOVAN GASTONE, 1671-1737
= Anna Maria of Saxe-Lauenburg, † 1741.

Anna Maria Luisa, 1667-1743
=John William of the Palatinate.

Above is the family tree of the great Medicis. The branch of the family tree from which Lorenzo descended ruled until the assassination of Alessandro de' Medici. Then the power was transferred to those who descended from Cosimo the Elder's brother, Lorenzo (referred to as the Elder). The last representative of the Medicis was Anna Maria Luisa, who died in 1743. She willed all of the treasures of the great family to the city of Florence.

Lorenzo's son Giovanni, who had become Pope Leo X, ruled Florence. However, after Lorenzo, none of the Medicis would come anywhere near to re-creating the great city that Florence had been.

IN CONCLUSION

The golden age of Florence came to an end with the death of Lorenzo de' Medici. Although he did not invent the Renaissance, Lorenzo's importance and influence cannot be overestimated. It was Lorenzo who was the Renaissance's greatest patron. Through his actions, the world of art was given such great men as Botticelli and Michelangelo. Lorenzo was not only a major influence in the field of the arts, but also drew politics, business, and learning together into the whole that was the Florentine Renaissance.

Although his reign as ruler of Florence was quite brief, the many accomplishments of Lorenzo the Magnificent during this time are quite astounding. More important, his influence has left a lasting impression on the way we think about art, the ways in which we are ruled, and the way we think about ourselves and our place in the world. Lorenzo was magnificent during his lifetime, and his legacy remains magnificent today.

TIMELINE

1348 The Black Death (bubonic plague) hits Florence.

1360 Giovanni di Bicci de' Medici (Lorenzo's great-grandfather and founder of the family) is born.

1389 Cosimo de' Medici (Lorenzo's grandfather) is born.

1429 Giovanni di Bicci de' Medici dies.

1434 The Albizzis are exiled; Cosimo becomes ruler of Florence.

1444 Cosimo establishes the first public library in Florence at the San Marco Church.

1449 Lorenzo de' Medici is born.

1464 Cosimo dies; his son, Piero de' Medici, comes to power in Florence.

1466 Diotisalvi Neroni attempts to overthrow the Medicis.

1469 Lorenzo marries Clarice Orsini. Piero dies; Lorenzo becomes ruler of Florence.

1470 Bernardo Nardi attempts to overthrow the Medicis.

1472 Revolt against Lorenzo in Volterra.

1478 The Pazzis assassinate Giuliano and try to remove Lorenzo from power. Naples declares war on Florence.

1479 Lorenzo goes to Naples to personally put an end to the war.

1480 The Ottoman Turks invade Italy.

1481 The Turks are defeated.

1482 Rome and Venice declare war against Duke Ercole of Ferrara. Milan, Naples, and Florence join forces against Rome and Venice.

1484 The Treaty of Bagnolo ends the war between the Italian states.

TIMELINE *[continued]*

1485 Pope Innocent VIII declares war on Naples.

1486 The war between Pope Innocent VIII and Naples ends through Lorenzo's intervention.

1489 The monk Savonarola arrives in Florence and begins criticizing Lorenzo and the morals of the Renaissance. His arrival marks the beginning of the end of Florence's golden age.

1492 Lorenzo dies.

GLOSSARY

florin The currency used in Florence.

fresco A style of painting popular during the Renaissance. Frescoes are created when an artist applies paint onto damp plaster made of ground sand, lime, or marble.

gonfalonier The highest-ranking position in the Florentine government.

gout An extremely painful medical condition that affects the joints; most of the Medici men suffered from it.

Greco-Roman The term used to describe something that is influenced by the ancient civilizations of Greece and Rome.

guild A group of businessmen from the same industry who came together to manage their particular trade.

humanism A branch of philosophy that focuses on and celebrates mankind.

Latin The language used in ancient Rome, as well as by schools, churches, and governments in Europe until modern times.

neoplatonism A branch of philosophy that tried to make the ideas of the Greek philosopher Plato correspond with the Christian religion.

Palazzo della Signoria The main governmental building in Florence.

Palazzo Medici The Medici family's palace and main home.

patronage A system in which rich people support, employ, and find work for artists.

Platonic Academy A group of artists, scholars, and philosophers who gathered around Lorenzo de' Medici during his time in power.

Renaissance A French word meaning "rebirth," which describes the period in history (from the fourteenth to the seventeenth centuries), when the works and wisdom of the ancient worlds of Greece and Rome were rediscovered.

republic A form of government in which the power resides in elected or appointed officials, who represent the will of the people.

San Lorenzo Church The church in which Lorenzo, and all the main Medicis, are buried.

San Marco Church A church that housed the Medici Library (the Biblioteca Marciana), the first public library in Europe.

FOR MORE INFORMATION

The Renaissance Society of America
Graduate School and University Center
City University of New York
365 Fifth Avenue, Room 5400
New York, NY 10016-4309
(212) 817-2130
e-mail: rsa@rsa.org
Web site: http://www.rsa.org

WEB SITES

Due to the changing nature of Internet
links, the Rosen Publishing Group, Inc.,
has developed an online list of Web
sites related to the subject of this
book. This site is updated regularly.
Please use this link to access the list:

http://www.rosenlinks.com/
  rsar/lome

For further reading

Caselli, Giovanni. *The Renaissance and the New World.* New York: Peter Bedrick Books, 1985.

Cole, Alison. *Eyewitness: Renaissance.* New York: DK Publishing, 2000.

Greenblatt, Miriam. *Lorenzo de' Medici and Renaissance Italy.* New York: Benchmark Books, 2003.

Howarth, Sarah. *Renaissance People.* Brookfield, CT: Millbrook Press, 1992.

Howarth, Sarah. *Renaissance Places.* Brookfield, CT: Millbrook Press, 1992.

Morley, Jacqueline. *A Renaissance Town.* New York: Peter Bedrick Books, 1996.

Nardo, Don. *The Italian Renaissance.* San Diego, CA: Kidhaven, 2003.

Quigley, Mary. *The Renaissance (Understanding People in the Past).* Chicago: Heinemann Library, 2003.

Shuter, Jane. *The Renaissance.* Des Plaines, IL: Heinemann Library, 2000.

Strauss Art, Suzanne. *The Story of the Renaissance.* Lincoln, MA: Pemblewick Press, 1997.

Wood, Tim. *The Renaissance.* New York: Viking Press, 1993.

BIBLIOGRAPHY

Ady, Cecilia M. *Lorenzo de Medici and Renaissance Italy*. London: The English Universities Press, 1970.

Hibbert, Christopher. *The House of Medici: Its Rise and Fall*. New York: William Morrow & Co., 1975.

Loth, David. *Lorenzo the Magnificent*. New York: Brentano's, 1929.

Mee, Charles L. *Lorenzo de' Medici and the Renaissance*. New York: American Heritage Publishing Co., 1969.

Roscoe, William. *The Life of Lorenzo de' Medici: Called the Magnificent*. London: Henry G. Bohn, 1846.

Ross Williamson, Hugh. *Lorenzo the Magnificent*. New York: Putnam, 1974.

INDEX

About the Author

Lee Hancock studied at the University of Gloucestershire in the United Kingdom, where he achieved an honors degree in history and religious studies. He has a lifelong passion for history. His previous work, *Saladin and the Kingdom of Jerusalem: The Muslims Recapture the Holy Land in AD 1187* was published by the Rosen Publishing Group. He lives in Worcestershire, with his wife, Donna.

Credits